From Telling
to
Teaching

MINNESOTA DEPARTMENT
OF HEALTH

Joye A. Norris, Ed.D

A Dialogue Approach to Adult Learning

From Telling to Teaching

Featuring a step-by-step
workshop design model
that will transform you,
your teaching, and
your learners!

From Telling to Teaching
A Dialogue Approach to Adult Learning
By Joye A. Norris, Ed.D

Packaged by: Pine Hill Graphics
Cover design by: Alpha Advertising

Published by: Learning By Dialogue
P.O.Box 3413
North Myrtle Beach, SC 29582
www.learningbydialogue.com

ISBN: 0-9729617-0-4

Printed in the United States of America.

From Telling to Teaching is dedicated to...

Dr. Jane Vella, my teacher, who lit this fire over a decade ago;

My family, which, while never really understanding what it is I do, cheers for me at every turn;

The thousands of frontline educators across the country who have encouraged me, inspired me, and lifted me up by their dedication to making a difference. To encourage is to "put passion in the heart." They certainly have put it in mine.

TABLE OF CONTENTS

Part I

*Laying the Foundation
for Teaching
Instead of Telling*

*When you, as an educator,
look into the eyes of your
learners, you are standing
at the gateway of enormous
learning capacity.*

Dr. Joye Norris

CHAPTER ONE

Why A Dialogue Approach?

Your brain is amazing. It is so good at learning that to *not* learn requires effort. It has a phenomenal natural memory that is soaking up data "24/7." Your brain is working night and day to make sense and meaning of new information. When you, as an educator, look into the eyes of your learners, you are standing at the gateway of enormous learning capacity.

One sure way to *not* take advantage of that capacity is to teach by talking at your learners. Sure, you can cover a lot of information. If you talk faster, you can cover even *more* information. You can create images and sound effects that are the envy of the slide show afficiandos. The fact remains that your learners learn best by getting engaged with the new information, by talking about, using it, making sense of it, and filing it in handy places for future use. They can process information on several tracks at once and can process words three times more

quickly than you can say them, leaving their brains plenty of opportunity to focus on things other than your information.

If teaching by telling ignores what we know about learning, why are so many educators still relying on telling?

- They tend to teach the way they were taught, and too many times they were asked to learn by being "talked at."
- Some educators believe it is their role to give the information and the learner's role to make something of it—or not. I refer to this as the "left to their own devices" model. Others call it "sink or swim" or "the bootstrap model."
- Teachers are sometimes under a great deal of pressure to "cover" a certain amount of material.
- Teaching by telling requires less preparation time.
- It's pretty scary business trying new teaching approaches, often without much support from colleagues.
- More and more, some teachers feel they must "teach to the test," and are facing learners who want nothing else.
- Teachers tend to teach they way they like to be taught, and if they prefer lecture…well, won't everyone else?
- If teachers don't care for small group work and interaction, they may assume others don't either.

A dialogue approach incorporates how adults learn best by combining the delivery of new information—what I call push—with opportunities for learners to do something with it. I call this pull. To take full advantage of the enormous capacity of the brain, though, push and pull aren't enough. Learning by doing—without reflection and transfer into the future—just doesn't have the impact of a more complete learning cycle.

Colin Rose and Malcolm Nicholl, authors of *Accelerated Learning for the 21st Century*, say that making personal meaning of new information is the central element of learning. A dialogue approach to teaching allows your learners to make that personal meaning and apply the new information and skills to their lives.

If you want more for your learners, if you want to hear less of yourself and more of them, if you want to have more fun teaching, the Telling to Teaching approach will liberate you and energize your learners.

Examine the journey we are going to take from this point. We begin at the beginning by addressing the learning climate. If your intent is to lecture and adhere to the "left to their own devices" model of teaching, then the environment may not be that significant. But if it is your intent for folks to engage in dialogue, try out new skills, and reflect on their learning, then the environment matters enormously. Learning begins at the door—not the desk. You will discover what you can do to shift the energy to learning.

Our journey then takes us to activating prior learning. You will find out about the powerful teaching practice of linking new information to what your learners already know.

Next stop? Learning style preferences. How easily we agree that we all learn differently. And yet so much of the education enterprise in general completely disregards these differences and continues to lecture. You will find out about your own preferences and how to address the preferences of your learners.

Our next destination introduces you to open questions—what they are and the role they play in a dialogue approach to teaching. My friend and mentor Dr. Jane Vella, author of *Learning to Listen, Learning to Teach*, tells us that if she could only teach one skill that would transform education, this would be it—asking open questions. Prepare to spend some quality time in this chapter!

When I use the word "dialogue," I am translating it as "words between us." So how does this happen? How can you get folks talking around the open questions? What if no one speaks? The good news is it's easy to get people talking by using partner interactions, trio talks, and table chats. You'll learn what they are and how to use them in this chapter called, "Open Questions: The Engines of Dialogue."

How can learning be reinforced during the lesson or class? How can your learners review information in fun yet substantive ways? How can you improve the odds that they will use the information or skill after they leave you? The chapter on reinforcement will offer responses to these questions and more.

When your journey has taken you through the power of reinforcing learning, you will be ready to start designing a workshop or a lesson or class. Nothing elaborate, mind you—just a good solid design. Let's get started on the foundation so you'll be ready to try your hand at design.

The folks who wrote
Quantum Teaching tell us
that learners will learn our
intent faster than anything
else we teach them. What
intent do your learners
learn so quickly from you?

Dr. Joye Norris

CHAPTER TWO

Setting the Learning Environment

The wise authors of *Quantum Teaching*, Bobbie DePorter, Mark Reardon, and Sarah Singer-Nourie, tell us quite simply that when it comes to teaching, everything counts. What your learners see, hear, and feel (and perhaps smell and taste!) when they arrive sets the tone for the rest of the session. You send a message to your learners which essentially says, "Welcome. I've been waiting for you."

Sometimes I think of this in terms of "company's coming." What do you do when they are? Tidy up a bit? Put out something colorful? Make up the guest bed with the new comforter? Put something on the stove that smells delightful? Set out fresh flowers?

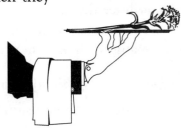

Quantum Teaching authors help us out again when they remind us that our learners will learn our intent faster than anything else we teach them. So what is the intent your learners learn when they arrive at your class or workshop? Do they learn that you are happy to see them, are excited about this opportunity, are prepared for them and recognize their potential?

Eight practices are standard for all my teaching opportunities. You can add to this list, I'm sure.

1. Ask for round tables so folks can see each other. Your high visual learners will be especially appreciative.
2. "Set" the tables. Put color markers and post-its in the center if needed.
3. Set your own table! Place a color tablecloth on your table and colorful baskets or bags. Make it as attractive as you can.
4. Arrive early for any session so you can have all the preparations completed and have time to meet and greet your learners.
5. Play music as folks come in—something that suits the occasion. The music serves as an alert to the learners. "This will be different!"
6. Provide name tags and ask learners to write their first name in large print. Use people's names immediately. They notice.
7. Make up welcome signs and place them where folks will see them.
8. Have all the materials prepared and ready for your learners. Give them what they need.

Remember, everything counts!

Setting a positive learning environment involves more than flowers and pretty colors. It is also about how your

learners will be treated by you and
each other. If you want people
to be receptive to participating—if you want them to
interact in small groups and
raise their voices—then you
also want them to feel safe to
do so.

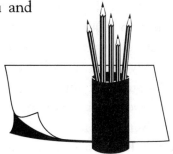

I set learner safety by:

- greeting people warmly as they arrive;
- asking them to help me practice the inclusion principle: welcoming any latecomers, telling them what we
  are doing;
- telling them I will not call on them nor go around the
  room for responses;
- letting them know I will wait five seconds for
  responses to open questions and that we will all wait
  for each other.

"Wait a minute…I tell them they
won't be called on? Then how do I
know they are paying attention? How
do I know they are learning?"

Ask any group of adults what they
most hated about school—at all levels.
Most of them will say, "being called on. I
was always afraid I wouldn't know the right
answer to what they asked."

This dialogue approach isn't about right
or wrong—it is about making personal meaning of the new
information. For example, a teacher could ask the group,
"How many servings of carbohydrates do we need each day?"
Or, the teacher could tell them and say, "Think about your

own life. What adjustments do you need to make?" The first question requires recall, the second REFLECTION. In this book, we're going to the second place.

My friend and adult educator Dr. Jane Vella captures this idea quite succinctly.

"Don't ask if you know the answer!"

Remember, when you ask open questions, your learners don't have to seek and find *your* answer—they find their *own*. You will be studying this idea more thoroughly as you progress through the chapters.

Setting a positive and safe learning environment helps you help your learners connect with the material both cognitively and emotionally. Why emotionally? Research tells us that people can remember and use new information more readily if it has been learned in ways that include the emotions. Recall some of your own learning experiences that you remember in some detail. Chances are they were fun, empowering to you, and connected to real life. You may have cried, developed new friends, risen to an occasion, achieved the unexpected, become "somebody."

It is difficult to connect with your learners when they are frightened or anxious. Think of the brain as having three lay-

ers—the brain stem, the mid brain and the upper brain. The brain stem is the center for survival and territory—not thinking. The mid-brain houses the emotional center. The upper brain is the thinking brain. When your learners do not feel safe, which part of the brain do you think they call into action? You're right—the survival part. I think of this as "down-linking." Build safety and rapport with your learners so they can work out of the emotional and thinking brain. Once you have established safety, you can challenge them to stretch what they know and to take risks.

Tell me a story, mommy—
and put me in it.

Family Circus cartoon
by Bill Keane, 1992

CHAPTER THREE

Activate Prior Learning

We learn best when we can connect new information to what we already know. I recall my own monumental struggle in statistics courses, set in motion by my very inadequate math background. How could I connect new information to—well—nothing? Have you had this experience? It is so much easier to learn when we have at least some familiarity with the subject.

As an educator, you can build in for your learners their opportunity to name what they already know,  and to begin to give their brain "addresses" for the new information. You can activate their prior learning. Here's an example.

The topic is Nursing Ethics. Rather than dive right into the subject, you ask your learners to do the following: "Find a partner. Describe to each other any situation in your life where you weren't sure what to do—one of those times where you felt 'caught between a rock and a hard place.' What did you do and why? How did it feel?" Perhaps you give them an example. After some time and a bit of whole group responding, you launch into Nursing Ethics. You have anchored the topic in the lives of your learners. Note the word "anchor." You'll see it again!

A *Family Circus* cartoon illustrates this idea beautifully. The little fellow is going to bed. His mom is tucking him in. He says, "tell me a story, mommy, and put *me* in it." (1992 Bill Keane, Inc.)

Find a way for your learners to activate their prior learning, to place themselves in the story. You can use warm-ups for the dual purpose of getting folks more comfortable with the class and for activating their prior learning.

Here's an example from nutrition education. The topic is cooking light for the holidays. You begin the lesson by asking participants to turn to another classmate and describe their favorite homemade holiday dish and how it was prepared. As folks share with the whole group their favorites, you can start making the connection to cooking light. You have brought them into the subject from their own lives. Our good friends who wrote *Quantum Teaching* tell us to go to their world first before bringing them to ours.

When you activate prior learning and experience, you help set a foundation for what is coming next.

I observed my friend Jane Vella at a conference that was kicking off a city-wide dialogue approach to education. She startled the 100+ audience when she began her session as follows:

"Turn to someone at your table and describe to each other any moment of dialogue you have personally experienced in the last two weeks."

After a moment of stunned silence, the voices began (raising all voices!) and the volume rose and the excitement grew and the energy rocketed skyward. Jane had not only "warmed-up" the audience—she activated their OWN experiences with dialogue.

Prior learning can be activated in as many ways as you can create. You've already read how simple open questions or phrases can start the ball rolling.

Read on to discover three more possibilities.

KWL

The KWL format is a popular practice for activating prior learning. (*Designing Brain Compatible Learning* by Parry and Gregory is one source for more information.) Quite simply, you put up a 3-column chart, labeled with a K (know), W (want to learn) and an L (learned).

Ask your learners to jot down on post-its (I always use colorful ones) what they know and what they want to learn and post their notes in the columns. They return to the "L" later to name what they learned. Don't feel limited to a chart on the wall. My colleague, Val Uccellani, draws a tree with limbs and ask learners to place what they know at the foot of the tree, what they want to learn on the branches, and eventually what they have learned as fruit!

Bingo

I teach a lesson about multiple intelligences—all the ways in which we are smart. Rather than beginning with a lot of information, I begin the lesson with a Bingo! It has sixteen squares. The instructions are to find someone who fits the description in each box. One box says, "can rearrange furniture and have it come out beautifully!" Another box says, "can sing the harmony just by hearing the melody." Throughout this short and lively bingo game, participants are finding out how many ways their co-participants are smart and telling others about themselves. The stage is set, then, for information about multiple intelligences. You can see a sample Bingo in the resources section of this book.

Passion Posters

Let's suppose the topic of your session is stress management. Place around the room large pictures or quotes related to stress. Ask your participants to stand up, take a walk around the room to read the quotes, then to stand by the one that most speaks to them at this moment. If this is a warm-up exercise, ask them to introduce themselves to others at their "post." Sample the group as to why they chose to stand where they did. ("Sample" means asking for just a few responses so you can keep up the energy and the pace.)

A bit more about warm-ups...

Warm-ups have been mentioned here in association with activating prior learning, but let's look more deeply into warm-ups themselves.

David Sousa, author of *How the Brain Learns*, tells us that the two most powerful learning times—when learners remember the most—are the beginning (most memorable) and the end (second most memorable). The primacy principle—or what comes first—tells us not to fritter away our beginnings! The recency principle—what comes last—tells us to close with strength.

You'll find many books containing dozens of "icebreakers," activities where participants get to know one another, get more comfortable, and get ready to learn. Many of these icebreakers have no relationship to the topic of the session, although they may be quite fun.

A dialogue approach incorporates warm-ups that are linked to the topic to some degree while accomplishing the "get to know you" and learner safety functions. The warm-ups take advantage of the primacy principle and they activate prior learning.

An example: Let's look at multiple intelligences again for an example of a warm-up. For the warm-up, before introducing M/I content, you could ask participants to turn to the person next to them and introduce themselves. Then ask them to describe what people say about particular ways in which they are smart or good or effective. One might say, "My best friend always tells me what a good listener I am," or "My mom always says I can find my way to any location without a map." Ask them to jot down these ways of being smart on post-its and bring them to charts so everyone can see.

After two or three minutes, ask for a few examples from the group. You may now introduce the concept of multiple intelligences. The warm-up "broke the ice," and got them thinking about ways of being smart.

Andy Bryner and Dawna Markova, authors of *The Unused Intelligence*, give us a delightful way to think about what we are doing when we move from telling to teaching. What's important, they say, is that learners leave the session knowing how brilliant *they* are, and not how brilliant the teachers are. When we activate prior learning, we begin with our learners' brilliance.

Your role as a teacher is to find as many ways as possible for your learners to show you how smart they are.

Dr. Joye Norris

CHAPTER FOUR

Variety Is the Spice of Teaching!

The traditional education practice of telling suits fewer than one-fourth of us. Psychologist Howard Gardner, developer of multiple intelligences theory, refers to the "single chance" teaching model. Listen and get it—or don't. We all learn differently and yet are treated to "one size fits all" teaching.

The "telling" approach to teaching is certainly the least memorable except on those occasions when we are privileged to hear a compelling speaker with a timely message. Examine the diagram or cone, introduced by Edgar Dale in 1969, in terms of how much learners can remember and use 24 hours after being introduced to the new information.

As a teacher you want to work your way—and your learners' ways—DOWN the cone!

WE CAN REMEMBER AND USE AFTER 24 HOURS...

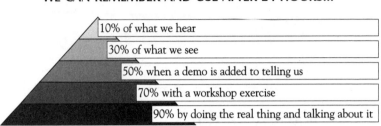

10% of what we hear
30% of what we see
50% when a demo is added to telling us
70% with a workshop exercise
90% by doing the real thing and talking about it

The top of the cone—where the least is remembered after 24 hours—features telling and appeals to auditory learners. As more visual components are added, recall goes up. As experience is added, recall soars.

Three Learning Modalities...
Visual, Auditory, and Kinesthetic (VAK)

Educators have been saying for decades that we all learn differently, and yet most education programs today disregard this fact. What about you? How do you learn?

Read the descriptions of three learning modalities—visual, kinesthetic, and auditory—and decide what your strongest learning modality preference is—hearing and saying it, seeing it, or doing it. These descriptions reflect several sources including David Meier's *Accelerated Learning Handbook*.

Approximately 60% of us have a strong preference for learning by seeing, which is not surprising given the extraordinary number of nerve receptors in our eyes. We are in tune with the visual aspects of everything—

the classroom, the walls, the other participants, and pictures, including the ones in our heads. The visual aspects of a classroom are what we notice first. "This *looks* interesting!" we may say. We often prefer to sit in the middle of a room so we can see all around us. We like round tables so we can see everyone and they can see us. We take notes and use them. We can recall page numbers and what section of a page contained certain information. Show us, we say. Draw it for us! Where are the pictures? (If you don't believe in the power of pictures, watch what happens to your lesson when someone starts passing around wedding photos! You're lesson is over.) In elementary school, the strong visual learners tend to be "teacher's pets," because they follow the teacher visually around the room and are viewed as being especially interested.

25% of us have a strong kinesthetic learning preference. For Pete's sake, let us get our hands on it and do it! We may find sitting and listening to be torture and enough already with the visuals. We crave experience and are impatient with the details. We are like the auto mechanics student who hates to read the book and much prefers figuring it out by doing it. We take notes just to be *doing* something, and not necessarily to use them in the future. The route to our brain is through our hands. Don't be surprised if we prefer the back of the room—either to fidget unobserved or to escape. Some of us may need to doodle in order to listen. We love cell phones by the way. Walk and talk and walk and talk! We are struck at the outset by the feel of the classroom, the arrangement of the furniture, the space or lack of it.

15% of us prefer learning through listening. We are struck upon entering a classroom by the sound of it, the conversations, the words. "This *sounds* like it will be interesting." We like lectures, words and debates. We enjoy discussion groups. We may listen to information on tape. We have big vocabularies. We usually sit in the front of the room so we can listen better. We aren't that keen on note-taking because

 it interferes with our listening. Oh, and you should know something else about the auditory learners, all 15% of us. Most of today's teaching is designed for us, *thank you very much*. Could you tell us some more? We can sit still and wait!

So, what about you? Are you strongly visual, auditory, or kinesthetic? You probably found elements of all three preferences that described you. Some of you are "teacher proof"— if you want it, regardless of preference, you will find a way to get it. You might read a book, watch a video, talk to someone else about the topic.

Your role as a teacher is to find as many ways as possible for your learners to *show you how smart they are*. You can do this by making your lessons very visual (my nutrition educator friends are great with props) and experiential.

If your learners can hear it, see it, write it, do it, say it…WOW! Colin and Rose tell us in *Accelerated Learning for the 21st Century*, that the majority of folks who do not complete high school are strong kinesthetic learners. Our school system is simply not equipped for them once they get beyond the earliest grades where kinesthetic is the order of the day. What audiences are you working with these days?

And by the way…we teachers tend to teach the way we like to learn, thus leaving out a lot of our learners. I have had teachers say to me, "I don't design for activities or experiences because I don't like to learn that way. But now I realize I have to get beyond my own discomfort. It's about them—not me."

Examples....

Incorporating all three learning modalities into your teaching is not as difficult as you might think. In my own practice, I find the following strategies very valuable.

1. Use round table seating. Let your learners see each other! For groups of 20 or less, use a circle arrangement some of the time and table work other times.

2. Make sure your learners can see you. A strong visual learner once said to me, "If I can't see you, I can't hear you."

3. Incorporate graphic organizers—visual ways of offering or sorting out information. I recently saw a design that used a poster of a traffic light with the red indicating "not good for you," the yellow indicating "so-so" and the green signifying "excellent!"

4. Get people up and out of their seats regularly. The longer your participants sit after fifteen minutes, the less they learn. I sometimes use a "carousel" format. Small groups of people—or pairs—or individuals—move from station to station or sign to sign or table to table—every two minutes. They may be responding to questions or a picture or a display or a problem. I use carousel music and say, "when the carousel starts, MOVE to the next station!"

5. Put something in your learners' hands. "Feel the three kinds of fabric. How are they different?"

6. Incorporate experiences that require working with the
   hands, such as sculpting with clay or building with
   pretzels and bread sticks.

A common response from participants in my training programs is, "But you don't understand. I'm not very creative."
You can find a wealth of materials in dozens of books from
which you can garner all kinds of ideas. That's your job.

A final note for this chapter about variety...

Eric Jensen, the author of
Brain-Based Learning, reminds
us of something quite fundamental and yet largely disre-
garded when it comes to
learning and the brain. For
crying out loud, whatever it is
you are teaching, try to make
it interesting! That's what the brain
most loves—something novel, something
different, something to get its attention. Even
the driest technical information can be made interesting.

If information is important,
provide it for your learners.
Why make them guess?
Instead, ask them open
questions about the information
you give them so they can
make personal meaning of it.
Why spend valuable time
undoing guesses when learners
could be doing something more
meaningful?

Dr. Joye Norris

CHAPTER FIVE

Open Questions:
The Engines of Dialogue

You've already read about the enormous capacity of the brain and the effort it takes to not learn. Well, something else takes effort as well: NOT answering questions. The brain, in its usual business of seeking something interesting, loves questions. " Ask me. Ask me another one. This is fun!" It automatically wants to respond to questions. Questions set thoughts in motion.

Have you ever been told something by someone who said to you, "don't tell anyone about this?" And sure enough someone asks about it and your body language betrays you because you have to fight with your brain to not respond verbally and you move your eyes to the side or up or down. So your questioner says, "I see. You don't have to say anything." You had already said it with your body. Why not harness this desire in a way that helps your learners become even smarter than they already are?

Four kinds of questions...

Closed questions are responded to with yes or no. "Do you have any questions?" "Did you enjoy your class?" "Did you learn a lot?" You can gather information with closed questions.

Recall questions "test" memory. "Who remembers why we need calcium?" "Which states border Missouri?" "Name the world's oceans." "Who remembers what we said yesterday?" Much if not most of today's education efforts live and die by recall or right and wrong questions. I personally lived and died by them in many of my own classes, relying on my memory when I didn't understand the concepts. Have you done that too? That method served me fairly well in some areas where memorization-type tests were the norm. That method failed me completely in math, since no amount of memorization helped me understand algebra.

Information questions have their place. "What is your name?" "How long have you been here?" "What made you choose history as a major?" Some "questions" are actually phrases or requests.

"Name two books about leadership for the new millennium." (recall)

Open questions or phrases cannot be answered with a simple yes or no. They take the learner to a deeper level, a more reflective place, a thinking place. They set thoughts in motion. They demand your learners' thoughts, not just yours.

"What do you believe any new book on leadership—to be relevant to our world now—needs to address?"

Notice the difference between the two leadership questions. One calls for recall ("Name two books...") One calls for thinking.

Don't steal the learning...

My friend Jane Vella taught me something years ago that it took me a while to understand. She would say,

"Joye, don't steal their learning!"

Steal it? How do I steal it? Well, one way I steal it is to ask only closed questions, seeking recall answers or yes and no. My learners busily "scan" my face, seeking the answer I want. My questions assume learners can't go deeper, we don't have time to go deeper, no one wants to go deeper, or there's no depth to this anyway! When I ask open questions, I assume folks have some neat thoughts of their own, that they can do something other than regurgitate facts, and that what they have to say is valuable. When I ask open questions, I energize learners' minds and help them focus.

According to Tom Wujec in *Five Star Mind*, the word "question" originates from the Latin root, "quaestio," which means to seek. The learning is in the seeking!

You read earlier that making personal meaning of new information is the central element of learning. Open questions and phrases allow learners to make that personal meaning. Here's an example from my wonderful breastfeeding support friends.

Option 1: When we began our class today, we reviewed reasons to breastfeed your child. Who can tell us what any of those reasons were? (Recall)

Option 2: Check your notes and find the reasons to breastfeed your child that we talked about when this class began today. Ask the person next to you, "which of these reasons makes the most sense to *you* now that you've had some time to think and talk about it?"

The first option required recall, the second required reflection or looking back.

Effective teaching isn't about right answers and wrong answers and "what do we do when they say THAT" answers, and "what if they don't say what we want them to" answers. If the information is so important, *give* it to them. Why ask them to guess? Why spend valuable time correcting what they guessed incorrectly? If the information is important, provide it for your learners, then ask them open questions about it. The *Quantum Teaching* folks call this making the invisible visible. If they need it, give it to them.

Some of my Kansas nutrition educator friends, after learning abut the power of open questions, told me they had begun taping possible questions on their teaching materials. "We found it hard to just come out with open questions, so we gave ourselves some support. It worked."

Check out this list of open questions and phrases before we move on to describing some exciting ways to use them. Read each one out loud. Get used to asking your questions in this way. You'll find more open questions in Part 3.

What questions do you have? (We assume they DO!)
How would that work in practice?
Tell me more about....(open phrase)
Why do you think that is so?
In what ways will this information help you in your life?
What do you think of....?
What other options do you have?
How could you handle it?
What information do you need to make this more clear?
Describe an example.
Tell us why that is important to you.

Good things come to those who wait...

As we close this segment on open questions, I must share with you the open question's best friend...*waiting for a response!* What good are your most carefully constructed open questions if you wait one second and assume no one is going to respond? I literally count out five seconds to myself and never cease to be amazed and what gets said at that point. You will find out more about the power of waiting in Chapter 12.

When partners speak with each other, all voices are raised. So is the energy. And on occasion, so is the roof!

Dr. Joye Norris

CHAPTER SIX

Partner Interactions

The word "dialogue" means "words between us." The word "facilitate" means "to make easy." Your role as the facilitator is to make those words between easy. How can you do that? How can you shift the voice from yours to theirs?

Earlier you learned about the importance of setting a positive and safe learning environment so that people feel free to speak. You read about activating prior learning and going to the learners' worlds first. You found out about the need to use a variety of approaches so people can show how smart they are. You examined the power of open questions and phrases to get people talking. Now you will look at some specific practices that will raise all the voices in your classroom, generate energy around the topic, and allow folks to make personal meaning of the new information.

The power of partnerships...

Put people into partnerships. Your learners benefit in three ways. They get to know each other. They can test out their ideas with just one person instead of risking their voice in front of the whole group. They also are lifted up by the growing energy in the room. I build several types of partner interactions into my training programs. Here are some examples.

1. **Howdy and a Quote:** "Howdy" works very well as a warm-up. Ask folks to stand, introduce themselves to someone in the group and talk about the quote you  have provided for each of them. The quote could be in their hands or on a name tag. The quote gives them something to talk about and the quote is related to the topic. At a recent training of trainers workshop, one of the quotes I provided was "Education is not the filling of a pail, but the lighting of a fire." You can create or borrow quotes **related to your topic** that help folks raise their voices and start connecting to the subject.

2. **Partner Interview:** Develop two or three questions for participants to ask a partner. Put the questions in writing.

    As a warm-up for a workshop on facilitation skills and a lead-in to the power of using names, I asked partners to interview each other and ask these two questions:
    a. Where did your first name come from?
    b. What do you like about it?

3. **Sentence Completion:** Ask your learners to complete a few simple sentences, then ask them to share their results with a partner. I've used this approach to introduce the idea of setting a positive learning environment. a) What did you notice first about this learning environment when you arrived? b) What most surprised you? c) What would you like to change? You have given the partners something to talk about—you have made words between easy.

4. **Verbal list and share:** This approach is especially useful when you are aware of literacy issues. Ask participants to verbally list something with a partner. For example, "describe to your partner five holiday foods that are especially important to your family!" The partner listens and then describes his or her own list. Again, you've gotten them talking in an easy fashion. Sometimes to illustrate the magnificent natural memory of the brain, I ask people to verbally list for one minute everything they remember doing, seeing, feeling, smelling, tasting, or touching on their way to this training room. Next, their partner takes a turn.

5. **Partner Circle and Share:** In a group of 8 or more, form two circles, an inner circle and outer. The participants face each other. Give them an open question or phrase and ask them to respond with each other. When the music starts, the inner circle moves around one person and the chatter starts again and continues until the inner

folks are back where they started. I use music to indicate that it's time to switch. "Circle and share" can easily become two rows of chairs with folks facing each other.

You are limited only by your imagination in coming up with partner interactions. By the way, the word "interact" means "to do with others." By using open questions, "doing with each other" goes much deeper. I was astonished at the power of a "two rows" partner interaction related to team building. The group members worked for the same organization. As their team building session closed, they faced each other in two rows and told what they really appreciated about each other. When the music started, one row "moved down" and the appreciation began again. The emotion and energy around this "raised the roof!" It reminded me of Jane Vella noting that the deepest learning takes place in the affective—or feeling—domain. To paraphrase a sentiment voiced by poet Maya Angelou, people may not remember what we said and they may not remember what we did. But they *will* remember how we made them feel.

Parker Palmer, in *Courage to Teach*, tells us that techniques are what we use until the teacher in us shows up. I

agree, but I also see partner interactions as something much more than a technique. A dialogue approach to teaching—a shift from the teacher telling to the participants talking—requires us to plan for those opportunities. The conversations, the interviews, the verbal listing—all allow learners to make personal meaning of the new information which is the whole reason to get away from teaching by telling.

Trio talks and table chats...

In some instances, you may choose to group participants in trios for a trio talk. I may use a trio talk when participants are practicing a skill with each other. The third learner is an observer with a specific role. I've used trio talks just to shift the energy in a room, to illustrate variety, or to get folks involved with more of their colleagues.

A table chat of no more than four can also change the energy and add some variety. Avoid table chats when each table has more than four participants because too few voices are heard. A table chat works especially well when the folks at each table are constructing a diagram or chart of some nature.

Don't be afraid!

I say this because the partner interactions and trio talks and table chats are the very heartbeat of a dialogue approach to learning. Coupled with open questions, these interactions provide the energy, the meaning making, the struggle, and the personal and collective growth of the participants and facilitators. These interactions bring forth the voices of the learners and shift the enterprise away from the teacher's voice. And yet, these interactions are the very first aspect of teaching through dialogue that facilitators drop. "Let's do this as a whole group since there are only six of you." Well, six people can make three partnerships or two trios!

Raise all voices.

When you teach, you are offering the vocabulary of the topic. The possession of that vocabulary is quite empowering. It is the key to the enterprise, the pass through the gates.

Dr. Joye Norris

CHAPTER SEVEN

Reinforcing the Learning

When learning is not reinforced, it can be quickly lost. When I think of reinforcing the learning so that folks are more likely to remember it and use it, I think about reinforcing language. I have come to believe that what we as teachers are really doing is teaching language. Oh, you didn't know you were a language teacher? Think about it. When you teach, you are offering the vocabulary of the topic. The possession of that vocabulary is quite empowering. It is the key to the enterprise, the pass through the gates.

Have you ever found yourself to be the outsider in a three-way conversation which is basically two-way because you have no idea what they are talking about? Why are you on the outside? In large part, it is because you are not privy to the language.

My stepson recently treated me to a tour of his Navy ship. It's entirely possible that I failed to understand at least 50% of what he was describing because of his easy use of Navy language. When he joined the Navy, he got access to their language and was using it with ease in very short order.

When you teach a subject, you are giving your learners access to its language. Rather than treat it as a given, treat the language itself as a powerful motivator and confidence-builder.

If you watch crime dramas on television, you know that the police and attorneys each have their own language. If you watch the medical dramas, you hear their language. Every topic has its language. So teach it!

You have begun learning the language of a dialogue approach to teaching, language that has certain meanings in this context. To reinforce your command of this new language, complete the checklist on the following page.

How much of the language of a dialogue approach has already become easy for you? It will be reinforced throughout this book so that it will become yours.

How can you reinforce the language?

Think of yourself in your teacher role. How can you reinforce the language of what you are teaching? We'll look at some possibilities.

1. Closings.

Remember the principle of primacy, that folks remember most what comes first? The recency principle states that people remember second best what comes last. Solem and

A Language Checklist

Examine each word or phrase. Next to it, place a check plus if you could teach it to someone else, a check if you have a good understanding, and a question mark if you need more clarification.

_____ 1. "Everything counts!" (*Quantum Teaching*)

_____ 2. Learning begins at the door, not the desk

_____ 3. Activate prior learning

_____ 4. "Tell me a story and put me in it."

_____ 5. Warm ups and primacy

_____ 6. Three learning modalities—V,A,K

_____ 7. Open questions

_____ 8. "Don't steal their learning." (*J. Vella*)

_____ 9. Waiting for responses

_____ 10. Partner interactions

_____ 11. To facilitate/to make easy

_____ 12. Dialogue—words between us

_____ 13. Reinforcing the learning/recency

_____ 14. The power of language

_____ 15. Raise all voices

Pike, in their book *Fifty Creative Training Closers*, remind us of the importance of closings to review information, tie concepts together, motivate, celebrate, or all of the above. Closings should reinforce the learning and the language. I design closings so that they require review of the language in interesting and fun ways. I have used a checklist for a closing by adding a partner interaction to it.

"Review the checklist. Mark what's clear to you and what needs clarification. Use all your notes. When you finish, share your results with a partner. Help each other clear up the concepts that need clarification. We'll address as a whole group whatever still needs explanation in five minutes."

This reinforcing closing exercise is not a test. Instead, it's a self-assessment combined with a little co-teaching, learner to learner.

2. Look back and bridge forward.

To look back requires reflection. "Looking back on this exercise, what most surprised you? What was the most interesting?" Remember, the brain wants to respond. In order to do so, the brain goes back through what it has heard and experienced. When you ask looking back questions, you help your learners deepen their understandings. Read these examples of looking back questions.

- What was the most difficult part of this exercise for you?
- What was the highlight of this training for you?
- Looking back on the four leadership styles, which one do you believe most closely reflects you?

Looking back questions reinforce the learning since the brain must review what it has learned and check out the connections it has made.

When you ask bridging forward questions, you help your learners take their new knowledge and skill into the future. For example, you might ask your learners:

- What is one new teaching practice you are going to try tomorrow?
- When you return to your office, what one thing can you change?
- When you go shopping for your family's groceries next week, which one of the ten smart shopping habits will you definitely try?

To reinforce learning, I often use a look back/bridge forward combination along with a partner interaction. For instance;

Sit with your partner. **Tell** each other your responses to the following two questions:

1. What part of our workshop on managing stress made the most sense to you?
2. What is one strategy you think will be especially applicable to your situation?

We'll hear some of your thoughts in the whole group after your chat.

Notice that the questions are *open*. They are not about right or wrong. Instead, they give learners space to apply the new learning to their own lives in their own ways. Also, the "play" with the questions reinforces the language of the topic. Your learners are thinking it and using it now, not in a hoped for future. I call this shifting from hope to evidence.

3. Language based games or puzzles.

A personal favorite closing exercise that reinforces language comes to us from Solem and Pike, *50 Creative Training Closers*. It's called "A-M, N-Z!" Teams of two learners draw out a chart with two columns, one labeled A-M, and the other labeled N-Z. When I say "go!" they fill in next to each letter a word or phrase that begins with that letter and that was talked about in our session. They may use all their notes and materials. Creativity is encouraged at all times and especially when they get to X, Y, and Z. I play feisty music in the background for five minutes or two songs. When the music stops, they post their results on a wall. If the group is small (less than 20) I'll ask them to gathered near the posters for a quick analysis. ("What strikes you about what you see? What did you have that no one else did?") Sometimes I'll ask for two volunteers to read their results to the group, again reinforcing language. The results are usually quite interesting and may give you opportunities to further strengthen concepts. The language of the session is reinforced beautifully. Everyone went through their notes again to fill in the spaces, the energy was high, and learning was fun.

I have used word searches to reinforce learning, again placing people into teams for safety and fun. You can create word searches using programs on the Internet. Just search for "puzzles" or "word search."

Additional reinforcement strategies...

You reinforce learning throughout the design when you engage your learners in auditory, visual, and kinesthetic ways. Information received through each modality is stored in different parts of the brain, making the topic more memorable to learners and more available. Suppose you are teaching the characteristics of effective leaders. You may tell your group what the characteristics are, show them pictures of famous leaders who exhibited such characteristics, and send them on a scavenger hunt to come back with objects that represent each characteristic. You have included all three modalities and made the information both memorable and fun.

We know that we learn through ideas, through feelings, and through actions. We reinforce learning when we design for all three domains—cognitive, affective, and psychomotor. Imagine that new moms have come to a class about handling fussy infants. To tap into all three domains, you can ask the new moms how it makes them feel when their babies are fussy. You can offer information on how to soothe babies. You can demonstrate how to soothe babies using dolls and then ask the moms to practice. By tapping into all three domains, you have reinforced their learning.

Congratulations! You have completed Part One of *From Telling to Teaching*. Part Two will walk you through designing for learning, using your new knowledge and skills to teach what you know.

Take a moment to consider this brief, look back/bridge forward transition to Part Two. The questions were inspired by Solem and Pike in *Fifty Creative Training Closers*.

Thinking back on what you have read and learned, what squares with what you already knew? What completes a circle of understanding for you? What has you looking at learning design from a new angle?

Looking to the future, what's one aspect of designing for dialogue you are especially excited about and anxious to put into play?

Part II

Lesson or Workshop Design

The teacher of a teacher-centered approach asks, "what do I need to do to teach this information?"

The teacher of a learner-centered approach asks, "what do they need to do to learn this topic?"

Dr. Joye Norris

CHAPTER EIGHT

The Journey Begins with Learning Needs Resource Assessment

A language check

As you prepare for a design journey, it's useful to re-examine what is meant by "learner-centered" and "dialogue approach." I call these concepts the "big idea," and have learned that they can get easily lost in the excitement of designing for learning.

A learner-centered approach isn't just a matter of asking your learners, "What do you need so we can give it to you?" It is a balance of meeting your learners' needs while *also* providing valuable information. Knowledgeable people provide important information to learners in a format that is focused on them, energized by them and made personal by them. The teacher of a teacher-centered approach says, "This is what *I* need to do to *teach* this concept." The teacher of a learner-centered approach says, "This is what *they* need to do to *learn* this concept."

A dialogue approach to teaching means that the air will be filled with open questions and responses among learners, that thoughts will be set in motion by words, that through conversation and wondering, adult learners will decide for themselves the meaning of new information and its importance to them. A monologue approach implies one voice—the teacher's—and right or wrong or recall questions with the meaning already determined.

Some folks see a dialogue approach as essentially a conversation. This conversation can be incorporated into groups of any size, by the way. Designing for dialogue is not limited to small groups. I have worked with groups that had over 300 participants. With some adjustments and careful planning, you can follow all the principles and practices of a dialogue approach. In this same spirit, you can adapt them to 1:1 teaching or counseling. As Bruce Springsteen sings it, no retreat and no surrender from words between us.

A necessary but not sufficient element of a learner-centered, dialogue approach to teaching is information. You will discover how to evaluate and measure out information so that it takes just one place at the dialogue table—not the only place.

Learning Needs Resource Assessment: Taking the "Pulse" of Your Learners

I attended a pre-conference session a few years ago called, "A Dialogue About Adult Learning." It was scheduled for three hours during a day that folks could have easily used for sightseeing in a lovely city. Instead, they came to this session expecting a dialogue about adult learning. Clearly they were interested.

A woman seated next to me introduced herself as an education professor from South Korea. With her was one of her graduate students. "We were so happy to see this topic on the program!"

The three facilitators introduced themselves as experts in public school education, K-12. Already the participants were a bit taken aback—but still hopeful. We were seated at round tables, the energy was high, and we waited for dialogue.

After nearly an hour of presentations by the three facilitators, the professor slipped a quick note over to me. "They do not know who we are." At that point she and her graduate student left the session at the break—as did many other participants.

In fairness, the facilitators should not have been asked to carry out this assignment. What stuck with me, though, was the message on the note.

How can you avoid your participants sending similar notes to each other, proclaiming that *you* do not know who *they* are?

You can conduct a learning needs resources assessment. You can "take the pulse" of your upcoming group. You can find out what energizes them, what their concerns are, what they do, how they do it, what they believe will help them, and what they will be bringing  to the group. A simple but powerful model for this "pulse taking" is suggested by Dr. Jane Vella in *Learning to Listen, Learning to Teach*. She says - ask, study, and observe.

ASK...

What can you ask and of whom to find out who your participants are, what they do, what they already know, and what

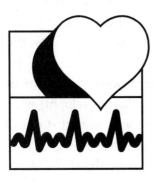

would build their capacity? I compose a few open questions and send them by e-mail if possible or ask the questions via a phone conversation. For example, I sent these questions to a recent group of 10 people who had asked me to guide them through a training design process.

1. What is your official role with this project?
2. What previous experience have you had designing and/or facilitating training programs?
3. What strengths will you be bringing to this program?
4. What do you believe would be the most helpful to you as you try to improve your designing skills?

I suggest a date and time for sending their responses. As responses come in, I reply with an e-mail and speak to at least one of their concerns. I don't need to hear from everyone—half will do. Remember, I am "taking the pulse" of the group.

If sending out an e-mail isn't realistic for you, find out who some key people are, pick up the phone, call them and ask your questions. They will be happy (and surprised) that you took the time to know who they are.

STUDY...

What can you study that will teach you who they are? Some examples include:

- Recent evaluation documents
- Surveys
- Final reports or summaries
- Program descriptions, mission statements
- Research related to their field

I work a lot with community nutrition educators, so I regularly read articles published in the journals that relate to their work. I want them to know I know who they are, what their challenges are, what kinds of questions they ask. The time you spend studying who they are will pay big dividends. You see, a training design is first and foremost an invitation. You are asking them to come with you. Only they can agree.

Observe...

Who or what can you observe so that you know who they are? Many of my participants over the years have come from the ranks of frontline workers who are doing the hardest work for the least compensation. So many times, they begin with the assumption that trainers have little if any idea of their workday, their realities, their victories and disappointments. They gamely prepare to adjust to this reality because it is the norm. Facilitators may not speak "their language."

What can you do? You can arrange to observe a day in the life of a participant. You can start learning the daily language

of their lives. You can spend some hours in a waiting room. You can accompany someone to a teaching assignment. You can find out who they are and where their strengths lie. They will thank you for making the effort and be more receptive to your program.

As you consider what to ask of whom, what to study, and what or who to observe, keep in mind these two key reasons for making the effort.

1. It is your job to connect with your learners in a way that they will say yes when you issue the invitation to learn.
2. The learning design you offer should reflect what you asked, studied, and observed so that it is relevant to your learners.

My colleague, a professor of nursing, asks her new students what they believe they are good at and what would make them better. The students write their responses on index cards and turn them in. One response struck a mighty cord with my friend. When asked about her strengths, a nursing student—Linda—wrote, "I don't think I'm very good at anything." My friend determined to look for an opportunity to alter that self assessment. Before checking Linda off on a particular skill, my friend told her how it would work, what to expect, what she would and would not have to say, and that she was safe to give it her best effort. The result was a perfect performance and appropriate praise. A few moments later, another student asked for assistance. Linda heard the request and said, "Oh, I can show her what to do. Is that okay?"

My friend had learned something important simply by asking—and it guided her teaching in a way that very likely changed a life.

Your turn!

Choose a topic you plan to teach or a topic that you've taught but want to redesign in a dialogue, learner-centered fashion. Keep it simple—perhaps a 1 hour lesson or workshop for 12 people. You be the judge.

Decide who you should talk to for needs assessment information. Develop three or four open questions for that purpose. Determine who or what you need to study and what you need to observe. I suggest you write all this out. Use the needs assessment worksheet on the next page for a template if it is useful to you. Remember, you are educating yourself about your topic and your learners' needs and strengths—the first step in training design. Your goal is to put *them* in the story.

Learning Needs Resource Assessment Worksheet

Your working title _____

ASK: First, name the people you want to question.

    Then, develop 3 or 4 open questions.

    1.

    2.

    3.

    4.

STUDY: Who or what could you study to assess your learners' needs and resources?

OBSERVE: What or whom can you observe to assess their needs and resources?

I've always known a great deal about my subject—but I haven't known how to teach it. What can you offer?

A typical inquiry

The Seven Steps of Planning

Joye's typical response

CHAPTER NINE

Seven Planning Steps That Will Change Your Life— Part One

Wow—I'm saying things like "change your LIFE!" Okay, I may be overstating it, but in all honesty, the seven steps I am introducing to you did change my professional life. They provided for me the missing ingredient. As a colleague put it just today, "I've always known a great deal about my subject but have found it a struggle to put it all together in ways that help others learn." The steps you are being introduced to will help you focus on what you are teaching and show you the way to design for doing. Remember, in a teacher-centered approach, you ask, "What do I need to do to teach this subject?" In a learner-centered approach, you ask, "What do *they* need to do in order to learn this subject?"

I am crediting Dr. Jane Vella for introducing me to these planning steps. She has described them in her books, including

Learning to Listen, Learning to Teach and *Taking Learning to Task*. My co-author Susan Baker and I described them in *Maximizing Paraprofessional Potential*. Today, the steps are coming to you.

Who, why, when, and where...

Did you expect something more complicated than who, why, when, and where? The simplest questions are often the most profound, such as "who are you?" Well, the simplest words—like who, why, where, and when—can be profound as well. Decide for yourself.

Who...

You've already read about the importance of knowing who your participants are. In this first planning step, you describe who they are - thinking in terms of information that will inform your design and make it relevant. You include yourself or other facilitators in the "who." You also include how many people will be participating.

Why...

Name the situation that calls for the training in terms of what learners need and want—not what *you* need and want. Sound simple? I find that most "why" statements are developed in terms of what the agency or program or organization must do—a teacher-centered approach. A learner-centered approach names what the learners need and want.

When...

What is the date and time of the program? How may learning hours does it contain? Include in the "when" the factors that may influence your design. For instance, perhaps what you are designing is the second of a three-part series. Say so! It will make a difference in your thinking.

Where...

What is the location? What does the training space offer? Does it have wall space? Round tables? Windows? Furniture that can be rearranged? Again, what can you say about the "where" that may have an impact on your design?

An example...

Follow along with a 90-minute workshop example that we will develop in Part 2, called *The Four Star Facilitator!* The following questions were sent to the participants prior to the training.

1. What is your greatest strength as an educator facilitating a dialogue approach?
2. What is your greatest challenge?
3. What do you believe would increase your confidence as a facilitator of learning?

Now, examine the chart on the next page and read the results of the first four steps in this plan—the who, why, when, and where.

These steps aren't necessarily written for your participants, although they can be. Their primary importance is to guide you as you begin the design process. When you walk yourself through these steps and record your decisions, you are giving yourself focus and thoroughness. The time it takes should prove to be worth it. I've worked with planning groups who didn't make it past the first two steps, who and why, learning to their chagrin that programs they had been offering for years lacked this level of analysis. They kept offering the programs thinking everyone agreed upon who and why, when in fact, they did not.

Seven Step Plan for the Four Star Facilitator	
WHO	45 frontline nutrition educators working with the Women, Infants, and Children Supplemental Feeding Program (WIC). They have teaching experience ranging from 1 year to 20 years. They have all recently taken part in a one-day training called A *Dialogue Approach to Teaching* led by Dr. Joye Norris of Learning By Dialogue. She is leading this session as well.
WHY	These participants spend part of every workday teaching classes to WIC clients. They want to be more effective educators by building better relationships with their clients and encouraging dialogue. While they are now familiar with the basics of dialogue education, they need more skills and confidence to facilitate the sessions.
WHEN	Tuesday, July 15, from 9 a.m.—10:45 a.m. 90 minutes learning time.
WHERE	A hotel meeting room featuring round tables, chairs, wall space, music, room to move around.

Give it a try. Go back to the topic you chose to develop and for which you wrote learning needs resource assessment questions. Walk yourself through the first four steps—who, why, when, and where. Be thorough. Make a template or worksheet such as the one on page 74.

Mark it with who, why, where, and when. You could write your responses on post-its and stick them on your chart. I personally like to design in big bold terms, using easels and flipchart paper. I can stand back and view the results. Sometimes I use quad-ruled graph paper and block out the steps.

Seven Step Plan for _____	
TOPIC / TITLE	
WHO (the participants and the facilitator(s). Includes how many.)	
WHY (the situation that calls for the session—what they need and want.)	
WHEN (the number of learning minutes or hours, the time of day, day of the week.)	
WHERE (the location, description of it.)	

We should typically be teaching half as much in twice the time.

Jane Vella and Joye Norris

CHAPTER TEN

The Seven Planning Steps— Part Two

You have now been introduced to needs assessment and the first four planning steps—who, why, when, and where. Before we walk through the next three steps— what, what for, and how—I want to give you one context that I use for the learning design process.

I view learning design as telling a story, one that has the learners in it. The story has a beginning and a middle and rather than an end, it has suggestions for the future.

You've seen that I use the term "journey" as well. When you design for dialogue, you take your learners on a journey. You make important decisions.

Where does the journey begin? Where does it go next? Why? In other words, you determine the sequence.

Are you ready to design?

What...

At the fifth planning step, you name what is to be taught. What knowledge? What skills? What do the participants need to know or know how to do related to this subject? Just as importantly, in what sequence will they best learn it?

This fifth step will likely take you more time than you are imagining now. Why so much time? Sometimes the hardest part of learning design is deciding what to leave in and what to leave out. It seems that we suffer from too much information and our reluctance to whittle it down. I have encountered this difficulty in every group I've ever worked with. They are always reluctant to give up "covering" a lot of information.

I see information as magic mix, a cornstarch, nonfat dry milk and margarine concoction my nutrition educator friends introduce to their homemakers. The mix will keep in the refrigerator for one month. From this magic mix, the homemakers can prepare all manner of food—muffins, pancakes, biscuits, pies, sauces. When you choose information for learning designs, you are essentially looking for the magic mix— the basic elements from which so much can grow. Let's face it. You can't hold on to all information and have any time for dialogue!

Another reason this fifth step can be tricky is that it requires you to not only name the content but to place it in an appropriate sequence. Remember the story? Where would it begin? Where would it go next? As you name the content of a session, you also choose a sequence. Once you have thoroughly examined the content and laid it out in a teachable sequence, you have done what my builder son does—you have built a firm foundation. If you don't get this part right, you are left with ongoing repairs!

An example:

Let's return to *The Four Star Facilitator!* Watch how I have named the content for that 90 minute session.

Extending the invitation to learn	Asking open questions	Waiting for responses	Affirming every voice

Of course, I could have chosen other content, but based on my experience, the group, and the time frame, I selected these four content areas—inviting people to learn, asking them open questions, waiting for their responses, and affirming all their voices. The sequence is by design—invite, ask, wait, and affirm.

The same content can be written in a question format.

How do you invite people to learn?	Why should you ask open questions?	Why should you wait for responses?	How do you affirm all voices?

I can also name the content as "How to" if that is appropriate for the topic.

How to invite people to learn	How to ask open questions	How to learn to wait	How to affirm all voices

In summary, I can <u>state</u> the content, put it into <u>questions</u>, or offer them as "<u>how to</u>" if the segment is skills-based.

Storyboarding...

Try using a storyboard approach. Remember the easel and chart paper I recommended earlier? You can do the same for naming the content.

STORYBOARD

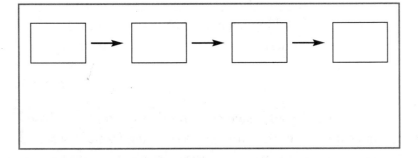

The best attribute of the storyboard method is that you can write your content on post-its and then move them, remove them, or replace them.

Return to your topic. You've named the who, why, where, and when. Now name the content on a storyboard—either a big easel and pad or on paper. You may also use the template on the next page which includes space for your content and for the next step.

Caution! Avoid the "too much information, too little time" trap. Take the extra time to examine content and pull out what is truly needed and what is not. **We should typically be teaching half as much in twice the time.**

Storyboard for Your Practice Session			
WHAT			
By the end of this workshop, you (the learner) will have:			
WHAT FOR (the next step)			

The template gives you room for three content segments which should be appropriate for a one hour session. For longer sessions, draw more boxes. The 90-minute *Four Star Facilitator* has four.

What for...

The phrase "what for" is Dr. Vella's language. It means, "what will they have done with the content?" Sometimes it's easier to think of this sixth step as developing achievement objectives because "what for" in this model is not the same as the broader "why" statement.

However you choose to think of it, you will soon discover that the inclusion of this sixth step is a fundamental departure from most training formats. Typically, folks designing curriculum say, "this is what we will teach and this is how we will do it."

You, on the other hand, will be saying, "This is the information they need. This is what they will do with that information, and this is how that will happen." You will have three steps, not two.

Link every piece of content to an achievement objective, using action verbs. You can have more than one objective for each content segment, but for now, stick with a one to one ratio.

Example: The content is <u>Extending the Invitation to Learn</u>. The objective could be, "By the end of this workshop, you will have **described** how you invite people to learn."

Notice that the objective is directly linked to the content name. Examine this storyboard that inserts all four content areas and objectives for The Four Star Facilitator!"

Four Star Facilitator Storyboard

Extending the invitation to learn	Asking open questions	Waiting for responses	Affirming every voice

By the end of this workshop, you (the learner) will have:

Described how you invite people to learn	**Developed** open questions for a lesson	**Created** a plan to improve your waiting skills	**Affirmed** responses to open questions

You will not be using language like "be able to," "have a greater understanding of" or "will have learned." In this process, your learners will be DOING during the session. *They will know they know.*

Imagine you are working with women in a family transitional shelter. You have 8 women who have expressed an interest in getting help completing job applications. You have been asked to design a workshop for them. You and they will have one hour.

Your learning needs resource assessment informs you that all of the women have filled out job applications in the past with varying degrees of success. They generally express a lack of confidence in the process. Walk through the first four steps—who, why, when, and where—each one significant in terms of what you design.

Now you are ready to name the content. What will you teach and what is it called? Break it down into parts. I imagine three parts and I'm calling them:

How are job applications a reflection of you?	What are the basic job application elements?	How do you complete an application?

I have many choices of content but am making these choices based on what I know about the participants and the subject.

The next design question is, what will these women have done with this content in order to have learned it? Examine my choices of achievement objectives on the next page.

Job Application workshop storyboard

How are job applications a reflection of you?	What are the basic job application elements?	How do you complete an application?

By the end of this workshop, you will have:

Named how job applications reflect you	**Labeled** the basic parts of an application	**Completed** a job application.

I now have the basic design blueprint for this workshop. The objectives were chosen because I believe if my participants accomplish them, they will know a great deal more about job applications than when they started—including having completed one. With this design blueprint in hand, I am now ready to address the seventh step. How exactly will they meet these objectives?

By the way, when I am uncertain as to what learners should do with information to make it their own, I insert a placeholder verb such as "will have reviewed" or "will have identified." I can go back and improve upon them as I get further along in the process.

Go back to your design. Develop achievement objectives for each content segment. Add them to page 81. Remind yourself that the objectives are *for your learners to achieve*, not you. Use the verbs provided here to help stimulate your thinking and to keep you focused on learning by doing. What action could they take that would most help them make personal meaning of the information or skill and transfer it into their lives?

Developed	Tasted	Identified	Separated
Decided	Traced	Reviewed	Critiqued
Drawn	Labeled	Analyzed	Prepared
Copied	Named	Examined	Used
Suggested	Applied	Built	Itemized
Created	Measured	Repaired	Fed
Sculpted	Drafted	Solved	Baked
Itemized	Constructed	Found	Illustrated
Cooked	Sewed	Chosen	Appraised
Compared	Saved	Replaced	Interpreted
Contrasted	Outlined	Called	Recorded
Explained	Ranked	Interviewed	Adapted
Defined	Sketched	Related	Matched
Written	Tried out	Bought	Indicated
Performed	Formed	Marketed	Practiced
Generated	Crafted	Edited	Completed
Rated	Recalled	Contacted	Redone
Evaluated	Gathered	Recorded	Mapped out
Selected	Listed	Played	Directed

How...

You have conducted a learning needs resource assessment, named the content and developed objectives. You now have a guide for your design. The question is, "how will this session be designed so that the learners will have achieved the objectives set out for them?" Osmosis isn't enough! You'll need to develop learning tasks. Again I thank Dr. Jane Vella for this language and recommend her book, *Taking Learning to Task* for a thorough examination of this concept. Over the years, I have used other language such as "activities" or "exercises." I have come full circle back to the language of learning tasks because the other two words just aren't big enough to capture what you are about to design for your learners.

A learning task takes content, grounds it in the realities of your learners' lives, gives them something useful to do with it, and allows them to reflect upon it and transfer it into the future. Examine this simple model for a learning task, suggested by my colleagues Val Uccellani and Cindy Bizzell.

A Learning Task Model

ANCHOR
Ground the topic in the learner's lives

ADD
Provide the new information

APPLY
Have learners do something with
the information

AWAY
Allow learners to move the
information into the future

A learning task does not have to have all four of these parts, but it does have to have application or it isn't a learning task.

These four parts can be seen as a learning cycle. By the time you take your learners through all four parts, they should have a pretty good grip on the new information.

Learning tasks feature open questions or phrases put to the learners along with the resources they need to respond. They should be easy to explain, have crispy, energetic language, and be doable. You need to design one learning task for every objective.

Let's return to *The Four Star Facilitator* 90-minute design. Here's the design "blueprint" or storyboard again.

Four Star Facilitator Storyboard

Extending the invitation to learn	Asking open questions	Waiting for responses	Affirming every voice

By the end of this workshop, you will have:

Described how you invite people to learn	**Developed** open questions for a lesson	**Created** a plan to improve your waiting skills	**Affirmed** responses to open questions

This workshop will begin with a brief welcome and overview so learners know what to expect. Since the title is *The Four Star Facilitator*, I might use star graphics to make the overview more visual.

I am considering the first content segment, issuing the invitation to learn. I am also remembering the power of warm-ups and activating prior learning, along with the effectiveness of beginning sessions with a partnering exercise.

How can this information become anchored in the lives of the participants? How can I give them new information? How can they do something with it? How can they move it into their future?

Examine this option which includes time estimates with some leeway.

Welcome and Overview: (1 Minute)

Task #1: Issue an Invitation to Learn!

A. **Listen** to these four snippets of songs. As you listen, **decide** which one best describes your teaching attitude. Turn to the person next to you to form a partnership. **Introduce** yourselves, and then **tell** each other what you chose and why. We'll hear some examples in the whole group. (A 6 minute ANCHOR segment including hearing examples)

B. **Follow** along with this brief explanation of the importance of issuing an invitation to learn. (Includes research, examples, list of strategies—captures the essence of the topic rather than all that is known about it.) (5 minutes of ADD)

C. **Examine** the list of strategies with your same partner. **Respond** to this question: What have you had success with that isn't included on this list? We'll hear some of your ideas in a couple of minutes. (6 minutes of APPLY)

D. Again with your partner, **decide** on a new strategy to invite your learners to learn the next time you teach. **Jot** it on a post it and **send** it up to our charts! We'll see what you decide! (5 minutes of AWAY)

Analyze the features of this learning task.

- It has a title.
- Part A (ANCHOR) functions as a warm-up that is directly linked to the topic.
- The task uses music as a way to engage the learners.
- It quickly raises all voices among learners.
- It features personal meaning, rather than right or wrong.
- It includes new information (ADD).
- The learners do something with the new information (APPLY).
- The learners move the new information into the future. (AWAY)
- The task is spelled out in clear language that is punctuated by action verbs.
- The whole group gets to hear and see some of the results.
- The new ideas that learners have are captured on post-its and could be sent back in a follow up report.
- The ADD component—the new information—is brief (perhaps 5 minutes) but solid.
- The task includes all four components of the anchor, add, apply, and away learning cycle.

A learning task does not have to include all four parts. You decide what allows the learners to accomplish their objectives in a sound manner.

A note about timing:

The Four Star Facilitator is a 90 minute session. It features four segments of new information and four objectives. In my mind, I am thinking of 20-25 minutes per segment, knowing that I will welcome the group and offer a quick overview before beginning. So learning task # 1 will take 20-25 minutes for learners to complete. I'm more interested in *pacing* instead of actual timing because in a dialogue approach, it's nice to have some leeway should the conversation get especially rich.

Ready for another example? Go back to the design blueprint for *The Four Star Facilitator* on page 87. The second objective says that learners will have developed open questions for a lesson. So how exactly will that happen? You're right—through another learning task.

Task #2: Tap The Power of Open Questions

A. **Listen** to this brief explanation of what open questions are and why they are important. These notes are in your program. (5 minutes of ADD)

B. **Think** of a dream you have for your life, large or small. **Stand** up! **Locate** a new partner. One of you **describe** your dream. Your partner will **listen** and then **ask** you three open questions about it. After 90 seconds, **switch** places! We'll hear in the whole group what discoveries you made about open questions. GO! (6 minutes of APPLY)

C. Take a moment to **reflect** upon any lesson you have been teaching. **Develop** two open questions that you could insert in that lesson to give it more meaning for your participants. **Use** your resource list to **stir** possibilities. **Write** it on a post-it and **share** it with your partner. Again, we'll hear a few examples in the whole group. (10 minutes of AWAY)

What are the features of this learning task?

- It has a title.
- It begins with the information (ADD). The information includes a list of open questions.

- Learners get to stand up.
- It has an application component where learners actually ask open questions and reflect upon their discoveries (APPLY).
- The application piece has potentially high energy because it is about them.
- The task closes with an AWAY component, asking them to develop a question they could use.
- It has plenty of action verbs and energy.

The third objective for the learners is to create a plan to improve their waiting skills. Check out learning task # 3 which was designed for them to accomplish that objective.

Task #3: Good Things Come to Those Who Wait!

A. **Watch** this demonstration. I'm going to ask the group an open question. Don't respond! {I'll wait five seconds.} What happened?

Talk to your partner about what happens to you or your learners when you are met with no response. We'll hear some examples. (6 minutes of ANCHOR)

B. **Follow** along with this brief explanation of the power of waiting for responses. {includes quote from Parker Palmer, the different ways people process information, the extraverts and introverts, plus ideas for learning to wait} (8 minutes ADD)

C. How can you begin waiting for responses from your learners as soon as tomorrow? What needs to happen? **Mull** over your plan with your partner. **Jot down** your two best ideas and **bring** them up to our Clock chart so everyone can benefit. (6 minutes of AWAY)

What are the features of Learning Task # 3?

- It has a title.
- It includes a demonstration.
- It is anchored in their lives, their experiences.
- Information is provided, including a quote and strategies (ADD).
- Participants get to plan for their own improvement {AWAY}.
- It incorporates a graphic—a clock chart!

The fourth objective for the learners indicates that they will affirm responses to open questions. How will that happen?

Task #4: Affirm All Voices So You'll Hear Them Again!

A. **Listen** to this explanation of why affirming all voices is such a powerful practice in learner-centered, dialogue education. I'll demonstrate some examples. (5 minutes of ADD)

B. **Stand up! Form** two lines so that you face each other as row A and row B.

You each have a list of open questions related to this training, and some examples of affirmations. Row A **ask** a question, row B **respond**, and row A **affirm**! Then **reverse**. When the music starts, Row A **move** down one space and do it all again. **Try** using the affirmations strategies listed on your question card. We'll hear about what you tried and learned. (10 minutes of APPLY)

C. **Conduct** a table chat responding to these two questions:

- What can you do to become more affirming of all voices?

- Name at least one other facilitation skill you plan to implement immediately and why.

We'll close with your ideas!
(APPLY, AWAY for 5 minutes)

What are the features of Task # 4?

- It has a title.
- It includes information {ADD} and an opportunity for learners to apply the information {APPLY}.
- It features an opportunity for folks to stand up, move, have fun. It incorporates music.
- It closes with bridging forward questions {AWAY}.

Glance at the four tasks again and note the shaded areas. Each of these areas represents the offering of new information. In this 90 minute session, the new information comes in at 25 minutes. It isn't just any information. It is key information in doses small enough to be engaging and large enough to be useful for subsequent application during the session. Only you can decide how much information is needed for your session. The key question is, *how much information do they need to accomplish the learning objective?* When you ask your learners to complete a learning task, it is your responsibility to give them the resources they need to do it.

Are you ready to write a learning task for your design?

Again you are encouraged to draw it out—write it out—make it big and visual. Remember to use partner interactions, trio talks, and table chats.

Return to your storyboard. This time, add the HOW or learning tasks. Write them *in the moment*, to your learners. What would you say to them? Describe to them? Explain to them? Ask them to do? Write it down in language that is to them, not notes for you.

Learners in my sessions have the learning tasks written for them, so they are seeing what I am seeing and can follow along. I like this approach because they do not have to ask for a lot of explanation, nor do they have to remember all the directions. They can refer to their own documents. You may or may not choose to provide the learning tasks in writing. If not, I recommend you back up verbal directions with charts, overheads, or slides. After all, you don't want learning to be sidetracked by participant confusion.

Beginnings and endings...

As you work on your one-hour session, think about how you want it to begin. A typical design practice for me is to use the first part of the first learning task as a warm-up element. In *The Four Star Facilitator*, participants assess their teaching attitude by listening to parts of four songs. In task # 4, the closing segment includes a bridge forward question that captures the whole session. Tend to your beginnings and endings—the two strongest learning times!

Check out the storyboard for a one hour session on page 95.

You will find another workshop example in Part 3, complete with learning tasks.

A Storyboard for a 3-Content Workshop

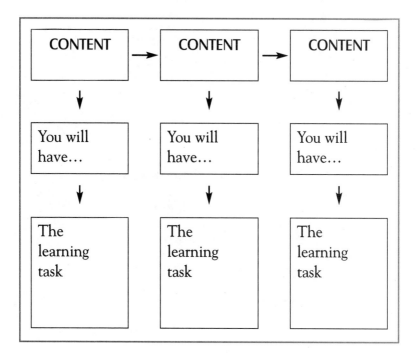

Your brain is primarily a visual processor. While 4/5ths of it processes images, only 1/5th of it processes words.

David Meier

CHAPTER ELEVEN

The Power of the Visual

You are already well on your way to designing lessons that are learner-centered and rich with dialogue. In Chapter Four you reflected on the visual and auditory and kinesthetic learners. Let's touch base on the visual again. Four/fifths of the brain processes visually and only 1/5th of it processes words.

If you don't believe it, consider how many times either you or others have said, "I never forget a face but I'm not very good with names." Well of course! The brain is such a strong visual processor, it captures faces into memory with relative ease. To remember names, however, requires an effort, several cognitive or emotional or kinesthetic steps. In my work, I have to make that effort to remember names. At the same time, I always ask that participants where big print name tags to make it easier for all of us.

If the brain is such a powerful visual processor, we designers of learning want to make learning as visual as possible. One way to accomplish this is to incorporate graphic organizers. They are already part of our everyday lives, by the way. Have you noticed the United Way "thermometer" that indicates how much money has been raised and how much more needs to come in? How about the newspaper, *USA Today*? It is chock full of colorful graphics that organize information for us, right down to the weather page. Nutrition labels are graphic organizers, capturing a graduate program's worth of information on a colorful label so small it fits on the side of cereal boxes. The Food Guide Pyramid is a graphic organizer. It takes reams of information and draws it out graphically so that the information is easily understood and used.

You too can graphically organize information for your learners so they can more easily make sense of it, use it, and remember it. Examine the follow basic shapes and consider how you might use them to organize information.

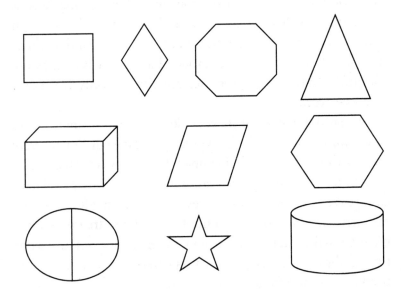

You can use objects—real or pictured—to organize information. A nutritionist chose the colorful image of a traffic signal to designate which foods were very safe for toddlers (green), mostly safe but caution required (yellow) and not safe at all (red). Another lesson from the WIC program features an image of stair steps to graphically organize infant development.

You can picture a project with three major components as a three-legged stool. You can use an image of a house and label aspects of information as the foundation, the siding, the doors, the windows, the walkway. You can organize information as pieces of a puzzle, slices of a pie, or layers of a cake.

Graphic organizers are also used to help your learners make sense of their own thoughts and contributions. For example, A PMI chart (Parry & Gregory, *Designing Brain Compatible Learning*) asks learners to name the pluses, the minuses and the interesting questions pertaining to a situation. A T-chart cold be used to help learners sort out their thoughts into two categories.

Remember that your role is to teach, not tell. It is to invite learners to make meaning and form new ideas, skills and behaviors to fit into their own context. Help your learners do that by incorporating graphic organizers. Return to the design you've been working on and decide where information could be organized graphically. Check out the next page for has more examples. You are limited only by your creativity.

Graphic Organizer Ideas

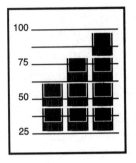

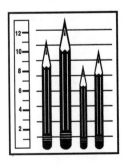

Without waiting, affirming, and weaving, the dialogue will quickly become a monologue, and the airtime will be inhabited primarily by you.

Dr. Joye Norris

CHAPTER TWELVE

The Fundamental Facilitation Skills for a Dialogue Approach to Teaching

Your journey through a learner-centered, dialogue approach to teaching has taken you through the fundamentals of design. You have one more "stop" on that journey, though—perhaps the most important one of all. This chapter introduces you to three facilitation skills that keep the dialogue afloat, that keep the energy in the environment, and that "connect the dots" for the learners. Without waiting, affirming, and weaving, the dialogue will quickly become a monologue and the air time will be inhabited primarily by you.

Good Things Come to Those Who Wait...

As you learned in Chapter Two, I let learners know at the outset that they will not be called upon and we will not go around the room. They have voice by choice in front of the whole group although small group participation is expected. I invite them to speak using invitational language. "Who would like to share?" or "I invite someone to give us an example."

Let's assume the questions you are asking are open questions. You've already learned about their power in a dialogue approach to teaching. Asking open questions requires its sister skill of waiting. I teach my students to wait five seconds for responses to open questions in the whole group. Amazing comments come forth right at that five second mark! I literally tap out five seconds with a finger or foot—ever so gently.

As I wait, I make eye contact with the "room," going from place to place, sometimes in an "M" shape. After all, waiting is not effective if I'm busying myself with my papers and charts and plans. I tell folks I'm going to wait for them right up front. Since they are just not used to this, it's common for people to start laughing after one second. Sometimes they nominate someone near them to speak, just to break the silence!

Within minutes, though, learners do become used to it. Reluctant speakers begin speaking. Ideas pore forth. I'm convinced those who are viewed as the "quiet ones" are so because the talkers have already taken the air time. Waiting five seconds allows everyone to at least think about what they want to say—or not say. Waiting five seconds allows learners to leave us believing they are brilliant and not that we are. If no one does speak, I might rephrase the question or, to their relief, move on!

Parker Palmer, author of *Courage to Teach*, shares with us what he realized about silence among his students. To paraphrase, he tells us that when his college students were not forthcoming with responses to his questions, he felt that something was wrong and that he had to fix it. He then filled the air with thoughts of his own. At some point he realized that they had no motivation whatsoever to dig a little deeper and offer their own thoughts. If they just waited, he would do it for them!

Look at the word SILENT. Now look at the word LISTEN. Do you notice that silent rearranged spells listen? Silence is really okay. Good things come to teachers who wait.

Affirming all voices...

So, the first learner has spoken in front of the group. What you do or say next will set the tone and your intent (remember, that's what they learn from you most quickly). A simple "thank you" is a good start. Adding their name to the "thank you" is also powerful, if not overdone.

Be careful to not issue too many "greats," goods," and "wonderfuls." Two reasons. One, if you always say this, your learners will give these comments little or no value. Second, the more reluctant speakers may vote no once you've pronounced someone else's comments to be the best idea you've ever heard! Thank them for their comment and then tell them WHY you're thanking them. "I'm glad you added that thought because it's an example of the importance of a healthy diet."

Some facilitators have fantastic eye contact, truly listen and care a great deal about what their learners are saying. But their learners don't know that, nor do other participants. I suggest that you give voice to affirmations, not just nods. Simple comments like "yes," "I see," or words repeated show the learner you are listening. Your role as a facilitator is to make dialogue—or words between us—easy. Affirming all responses is part of that role.

Weaving...

You were introduced to the power of language in previous chapters. You also draw on that power to weave a workshop together, to verbally review what was said or what is coming next, to make transitions from one place to another, to assist the journey. In a dialogue approach, where voices fill the air and the energy rises and the effect of being listened to takes hold, the conversation can drift or take different directions. You use weaving language to "gather it back up." It might sound like this.

"We've heard so many great examples of adults as decision makers in their own learning. Hold those examples in your hearts and minds as we begin to examine some classroom strategies."

You become the "thread" that holds the tapestry together.

Use weaving language to review concepts, tie things together, motivate, or celebrate. What you say matters. As our *Quantum Teaching* friends tell us, everything counts.

Congratulations! You have completed Part One and Part Two of *From Telling to Teaching*. I encourage you to put into practice your new knowledge and skills—and your new attitude about teaching. Let *From Telling to Teaching* be the "magic mix" for your development as a four star learning designer and facilitator. Hundreds of resources are available to you. Some of my favorites are included in Part Three. The added benefit of becoming a designer of dialogue education is that you will have so much more fun! When you use a dialogue approach to learning design, you have the power to transform yourself, your teaching, and your learners.

To encourage is to put passion in the heart. I hope *From Telling to Teaching* has added passion to yours.

Part III

Resources

Multiple Intelligence Bingo

Find someone who...

Thinks decorating a room is easy and fun	Likes puzzles that require reasoning	Easily remembers song lyrics	Enjoys outdoor games and sports
Records thoughts and feelings in a personal journal	Enjoys viewing art masterpieces	Learns best when emotionally attached to the subject	Is interested in biology and botany or zoology
Can easily sing the harmony to a melody	Benefits from study groups	Likes to work in a garden	Wonders what our place is in the universe
Has a sixth sense about the weather and seasonal changes	Engages in arts and crafts	Knows how to get back to locations without a map	Gets frustrated with unorganized people

You can use a bingo for your topic and set your own rules.

Books Cited in *From Telling to Teaching*

Bryner, A., & Markova, D. (1996). *An Unused Intelligence*. California: Conari Press.

DePorter, B., Reardon, M., & Singer-Nourie, S.(1999) *Quantum Teaching*. Massachusetts: Allyn and Bacon.

Jensen, E. (2000). *Brain-Based Learning*. Illinois: Skylight Publishing.

Meier, D. (2000). *Accelerated Learning Handbook*. Massachusetts: Allyn and Bacon.

Norris, J., & Baker, S.(1999). *Maximizing Paraprofessional Training*. Malabar,FL: Krieger.

Palmer, P. (1998). *The Courage to Teach*. San Francisco: Jossey-Bass.

Parry, T., & Gregory, G. (1998) *Designing Brain Compatible Learning*. Illinois: Skylight Publishing.

Rose,C. & Nicholl, C. (1997). *Accelerated Learning for the 21st Century*. New York: Delacorte Press.

Solem, L., & and Pike, B. (1997). *Fifty Creative Training Closers*. San Francisco: Pfeiffer/Jossey-Bass.

Sousa, D. (2001). *How The Brain Learns*. Thousand Oaks, CA: Corwin Press

Vella, J. (2002). *Learning to Listen, Learning to Teach*. San Francisco: Jossey-Bass.

Vella, J. (2000) *Taking Learning to Task*. San Francisco: Jossey-Bass.

Wujec, T. (1995). *Five Star Mind*. New York: Doubleday.

Additional Resources for Enrichment and Learning Task Ideas

Bellenca, J. (1997). *Active Learning Handbook for Multiple Intelligences.* Illinois: Skylight Publishing.

Bowman, S. (1999). *Shake, Rattle, and Roll.* Nevada: Bowperson Publishing. (Each of Sharon's books is chock full of ideas!)

Hannaford, C. (1995). *Smart Moves: Why Learning Is Not All In Your Head.* Atlanta, GA: Great Ocean Publishers.

Jensen, E. (1998). *Trainers Bonanza.* San Diego, CA: The Brain Store.

Jensen, E. (2000) *Learning With The Body in Mind.* San Diego, CA: The Brain Store.

Silberman, M. (1996). *Active Learning: 101 Strategies to Teach Any Subject.* Massachusetts: Simon and Schuster.

The Internet : Type in Accelerated Learning, Multiple Intelligences, Brain Based Learning—and reap the rewards.

Global Learning Partners, founded by Dr. Jane Vella, offers four-day courses in basic and advanced dialogue design. Their website is www.globalearning.com

Word puzzles are available at qualint.com.

Open Questions and Phrases:
The backbone of a dialogue approach to teaching!

In what ways can you...?

Describe what you see...

What are some examples of...?

What was the most valuable part of...?

What surprised you about...?

Why are you surprised?

What are you really excited about?

What is the best thing that could happen?

What would you do if...?

How could you improve this situation?

What do you need to ask to make this more clear?

How can you remember this?

What do you think of when...?

How are they different?

What could you do to...?

What happens when...?

What are your questions?

Tell me more about...

What do you make of...?

What is your take on...?

Describe your solution...

What would you add to this list and why?

How will this information change your life?

How would you rewrite this?

What's one thing you can change?

Sample Lesson: Power Up Your Mind!

This is a 50-minute workshop for a group of 30-40 people. New content areas are shaded in gray. The open questions or phrases are underlined for you so you can see the role they play in this design.

WHAT	Why Your Brain Needs Energy	Brain Draining Eating Habits	Brain Boosting Eating Strategies
WHAT FOR: By the end of this workshop, you will have:	Assessed your own brain's need for energy	Examined your brain draining food habits	Developed a plan to boost your brain power!

Welcome and Overview (could be done graphically)

Task # 1. Getting Acquainted With Your Brain! (total 15-20 mins.)

   A. **Describe** to a partner <u>how you know when your brain is in need of a boost!</u> We'll hear some examples. (ANCHOR)

   B. **Listen** to this description of your brain's need for quick fuel. (ADD)

   C. **Tell** your partner what you typically do to energize <u>your brain</u>. Based on what you just learned, <u>what's something you already know you want to change?</u> (APPLY)

Task # 2. How You Drain Your Brain's Power
(Total: 15-20 mins.)

A. Follow along with this fascinating information about
   how we do damage to our brain's energy. (ADD)
   (Lots of visuals, recent information on dieting and the
   brain, the impact of coffee, memory problems)
   What are your questions?
B. With your partner, **complete** your checklist of brain
   draining eating and drinking habits. Be honest!
   <u>Which of these habits are part of your lives?</u> Why?
   We'll all hear some of your discoveries. (APPLY)

Task # 3. Power Up Your Brain With Better Habits!
(Total: 15-20 mins.)

A. **Turn** to your Power Up Your Brain chart and follow
   along as you hear about boosting iron, taking B vita-
   mins, and improving your brain diet! (ADD)
B. With a partner, **examine** your Brain Power chart.
   Determine <u>what makes the most sense to you based
   on your own experiences.</u> Then, <u>what most surprises
   you?</u> We'll hear your thoughts in a couple of minutes.
   (APPLY)
C. To close this session, **take** your post-it notes. With a
   dark marker, **jot** down <u>two changes you plan to make
   right away to boost your brain power.</u> **Bring** your notes
   to our Brain Power chart so everyone can share in the
   excitement! (AWAY)

The areas shaded in gray are the content areas, or the ADD in anchor, add, apply, and away. The content is taken down to its essentials. Throughout this design, learners make personal meaning of the new information. They achieve the objectives. Task # 3 concludes with a bridge forward partner interaction. Not only have the learners made personal meaning of the information during the session, but they have also planned to take the information into their futures. You and they know they know.

Dr. Norris's dynamic, motivating, and immediately applicable training programs may be just the ticket for your organization—particularly if you desire better outcomes for your learners and more satisfaction among your teachers or trainers.

She is available for conference programs, workshops, training of trainer courses, curriculum design, and facilitation skills training. Program titles include "Teaching So They Will Remember," "Raising All Voices: A Dialogue Approach to Education," and "The Five Star Facilitator." In addition to coming to your location, Dr. Norris teaches a customized two or three day version of From Telling to Teaching to individuals and small groups in North Myrtle Beach, SC (at the Suncoast Adult Learning Center).

You can find more information about Dr. Norris and Learning By Dialogue by going to www.learningbydialogue.com. Contact her at info@learningbydialogue.com or 843-281-8832.

INDEX